My Name Is Pronounced Holy

A COLLECTION OF POEMS, PRAYERS, REMEMBERINGS, & RECLAMATIONS

Sha'Condria Sices-Sibley

"...and I wanted to hear those simple religious songs, those simple prayers — that true devotion...
And I wanted to hear that Louisiana dialect —
that combination of English, Creole, Cajun, and Black.
For me there's no more beautiful sound anywhere—"

—Ernest Gaines

for all the Ones searching desperately for a name
they have never really forgotten.

Published by Nine Pages Media
asiarainey@gmail.com
www.ninepagesmedia.com

Cover Design by odDbutCoMplete

ISBN: 978-1-7364659-0-5

My Name Is Pronounced Holy |

Processional | 1

Recessional | 66

Processional|

"We were made in His image, then call us by our [name]."
—Erykah Badu

Names that are created from unknown origins and erased histories usually can't be found among souvenir keychains, airbrushed t-shirts, engraved keepsakes, or even most books. I grew up in what some would call "the country"—"a little Blk girl with a big name" from a small town and descendant of the kind of resilient, resourceful, regal (and highly religious) people who actually built just about everything *this* country tries to call its own. The kind of folks whose names have been erased from records, history, and many times, our own memories. The kind of people who had no say in their migration to this land (also, the kind of people who were *already* here). Who were stripped of everything down to their names and the names they called their God. Who were branded with others' shameful last names but took the scars and gave them pride. Who had to make a home out of *stolen*, not with what could fit in a suitcase or bag or even on their backs, but only with whatever they could still protect and fight to keep.

Besides Arna Bontemps, I can't really name many (correction: *any*) writers from my lil hometown of Alexandria, Louisiana—let alone any Blk writers, let alone any Blk women writers, let alone any Blk women writers with a name like mine. There is something laborious *and* liberating about carrying a name like *Sha'Condria* that causes you to become aware of the weight, as well as the attempted erasure, of your existence.

You learn to listen, to watch, to not only hear, but also to read lips and the true meaning and intention behind what others choose and choose *not* to say, including your name. You watch as people's mouths willingly (and accurately) hold other multisyllabic names yet surrender lazily at even the thought of [up]lifting a name like yours. To preserve yourself—your life, your humanity, and your legacy—you learn to become adamant and unflinching about teaching people what *and* how to call you. I learned very early the significance of a name, but more important, the gravity of what it is you answer to.

In "remembering" these words—the words on these pages—I am taking a journey across oceans of submerged things that I, as a Blk southern Woman and writer, and those of my tribe were forced to forget (and other things that we wish we could), realizing that our prayers, our stories, our memories, our songs, our names just *may* be hard to say if a tongue is too frail to carry their heaviness, and thus, their power. Or too stiff to keep up with our immortal rhythm. Besides, this book ain't for them no way. It is instead a reminder, a keepsake, to myself and to those of us who had/have to reach deep down into the core of ourselves and learn *bloom* in this soil. For us to not only remember our own names, but to speak them with reverence and boldness every day; and when need be, to correct *anyone* who tries to call our names anything other than *Holy*, "to say it right or don't say it at all."

When The Battle Is Already Won |

"A bill is coming in that I fear America is not prepared to pay... a vengeance that does not really depend on, and cannot really be... prevented by any police force or army: historical vengeance, a cosmic vengeance..."
—James Baldwin, *The Fire Next Time*

I'm not sure if we have (in our possession)
the artillery to shoot our way out of this one
either
despite what the media say,
despite what the police reports say,
despite what the empty shell casings
next to playgrounds
in hoods that we only own the nicknames to
say,
despite what hate-twisted mouths say
when accountability is aimed their way.

They all rumor that, surely,
we *must* have enough ammunition to fuel an arsenal
of weapons we didn't invent
in wars that we didn't
either;
especially considering our decades of experience
in witnessing, then burying the carnage
after Baghdad has been bundled into bars
and bricks
and hand-delivered to our blocks.

We *must* be resourceful enough, considering all
the training we have had
in how to stretch minimum wage pay
or no pay at all
into enough to barely cover rent
and *still* have enough fingernail
and grit
to scrape up the rest
to ship our children's evicted bodies *Home*.

Surely,
we *must* be a prepared people after centuries of fighting
just to remember
how this fight even started in the first place
        and, now that it has...
that the opposing side looks nothing like
each other;
even though target practice can camouflage
as simply doing what we can
to blast our way out of the trenches,
sometimes hitting what/
whoever
happens to be in the way.

One thing, of which I am almost certain,
however,
is that to walk out of this blaze
victorious,
we never needed *any* kind of man-made firepower
to begin with.

If we did, I have faith
that we would have far *more than enough*
                        already.

Muse |

Somewhere
in a lil town like mine
in a 'hood like mine
on a street like mine
in a House like mine...

maybe, there is a Girl
with simple words and a complex
Name who needs to see another Name
that look like it could be *Her*
> Mama's or *Her*
> Sister's or *Her*
> Auntie's or *Her*
> Cousin's or *Her*
> Best-Friend's
> > or *Her|*'s

when she searches for something family[ar]
across rows and rows and rows...
down spines and spines and spines...
between pages and pages and pages...
within lines and lines and lines...
> of Names that are stingy with syllables
> or Names that are no louder than a respectable tone
> or even Names that broke through the dirt
> of *any* other country
> > but *Here*—

> *any* Names other than the Ones
that, in sea/ sickness,
were vomited up on these shores

and washed away more and more with each ravenous
tide;

any Names other than the Ones
who called this *Home*
long before thieves picked the locks,
set up shop,
            and changed it to America.

Maybe she a Country
girl from country folk
with dis   -   membered knowledge of *Her*
        origin before *Her*
                Big Daddy, *Her*
                Madear, and God,
                        maybe.

Much of Her lineage lies scattered Somewhere beneath
a maze
of headstones in the *Garden (of Memories)*—
a place with too many
            flowers and not enough re-membering;

or beneath rows of crooked crosses
in overgrown churchyards
on now abandoned roads—

Somewhere

in Alexandria,
Somewhere in Boyce,
Somewhere in Taylor Hill,
Somewhere in Hannah,
Somewhere in Three League,
Somewhere in Powhatan,

Somewhere in Many,
Somewhere in the middle
        of *only-God-knows-where*;

Somewhere,

where entire villages and towns full of Names & Faces
& Stories hopped into the casket too
when Such N. Seaux died.
Somewhere
        in the whole wide Country,

maybe there is a Girl
who don't know nothin 'bout *Her*
could be West African or *Her*
could be Caribbean or *Her*
could be part "Indian" or *Her*
could be nothin else
but *Her*
        fasho "Blk."

She who only got faith in a God she can feel
but can't quite name
and both of her Grandmamas'
faith in Jesus and prayer.

She who is of Those who tucked their dreams
reverently between
the pages of dog-eared daily devotionals
                        and superstition.

She who knows Psalms & Proverbs
  and salt & shoulders,
knows fire & brimstone
  and spit & brooms,
knows wine & wafers
  and cracks & Mamas with damn-near broken backs.

She who is tender
mustard greens & hotwater cornbread
crafted in hand-me-down cast iron skillets
and skillfully eaten with fingers instead of forks,
because she was taught that we already came here with
everything
we need (and... it just tastes better that way).
She who is homemade butter biscuits
  & mudpies
   & *Everything*
  southern&deep&brown
   & made lovingly by Hand.

Maybe,

She needs to see a familiar Face
a familiar *Name*
a familiar Story
about how something so *living*
can grow from the same kind
of Stolen/
  land.

I Was Born By... |

a (Red) River
in a charity hospital
named after a former Louisiana governor who drowned
in a sea of his own blood
on the same date, 45 years before
my mother's 15-year old belly
became a parted body
of water;

a Boot
in a place where concrete feet sink
(un)comfortably into "steel toes."

a Paper Mill
Churning out rumors beneath a veil
of smoke,
where you are only one church member
away from becoming the *Talk* of the *Town*,

a Prayer
where every ear got an open mouth, hungry
for the Good Word *and* the bad news
and a sticky tongue that stay on ready
to lick a stamp and send both clean
across town before you can put your hands together
to say *"Thank you, Lord."*

a Parish
Named Rapides: a French word meaning *rapids*,
meaning *a river somewhere between a run and a cascade*,
between a smooth flow and a waterfall;
a steady stream

where nothing and nobody is in a rush—
a gentle pulse

a Heart
smack dab in the center of Louisiana's chest,

a Storm
a state with hurricanes parading through its veins.
And here be the (seemingly) calmest part, the eye,
where folks got the magical and meteorological ability
to look right at yo' face
and predict the path you must have traveled—
your family's last name or what side of town you from:
> *Who yo' people?*
> *What's yo mama/ daddy name?*
> *Cuz you look just like one o' them*
> _____s

a 'Hood
> *out the Sonya Quarters,*
> *from that 'Nawfside,*
> *Kellyland,*
> *Karst Park,*
> *Evergreen,*
> *Deerfield,*
> *Martin Park,*
> *Samtown,*
> *Acadian Village...*

a Tree
where Somebody wanna stretch into a world
beyond the CenLa shade and so
many more do not.
Especially in a place that feels too much like deeply-
rooted.

Especially in a place with so many tangled branches
keeping you planted.
Where families be big like Daddy's appetite/Love;
and everybody got beaucoup cousins,
especially on they mama side—

a Cloud
one fluffy forearm floating above her hip.
Keep a Newport and the New Testament
dangling from her bottom lip
'cause she gon serve the good Lord until her very last breath
and she finally see Heaven for herself.

a Garden
Here, the men have tongues and hearts
heavy as shovels.
Grandmamas know dig/pile.
Granddaddies know dirt/plant.
And the seeds take and bury it all
and try to stand on top
just to keep their heads above ground.

a Mirror
where every Body wears too well
both the gospel and the blues.
Will chop and screw it, jig and zydeco to it.
Where uniforms (usually consisting of church clothes
      or work clothes
      or a crisp white tee
      or a Polo and Levi's,
      starched and creased,
      sharp enough to cut cornbread)
are a look
that ain't never goin' out of style;

a Machine

neither is being Baptist and baptized
in fifths of E&J, tall cans of Keystone Light,
and a blanket of Black & Mild and reggie smoke,
clogging arteries and atmosphere
like the exhaust of an old school American-made car
       (a big body Chevy,
          a Buick drippin candy all over the pavement,
          an Oldsmobile sittin on rims worth more
               than than the whip itself,
         a 'Lac leaning like lazy elbows)
bending corners,
always headed somewhere
or sometimes, nowhere at all.

a Bridge

Rarely destination to travelers
but merely a place they have passed through
(or across).
Where folks bend over backwards
to keep from drowning
and hold each other's hand
to keep from falling down.

a Welcome

Here, the babies come early.
The old people stay long.
And the doors of the church
and the corner store
are always open.

Make It to Heaven That Way |

You ain't neva received an invitation
til the doors of a Louisiana cookout
      or barbeque
      or crawfish boil
      or trail ride
      or fish fry
have been opened unto you.

Especially on the kind of summer day that
sticks to your flesh like sin—
the kinda day when every Body backslides,
going back and forth between
fanning flies and mosquitoes *away*
and any cool breath God can spare *in*.

Ain't no fancy gold trays laid out on pressed,
lamb's white tablecloth, instead
Communion be served on a spread of
paper plates and plastic/styrofoam cups
stacked on top of a card table
(that is still here only by the grace of God).

And we do this in Remembrance of
everything we be tryna forget

from the day
the week
the year
or the lifetime before.

After thanks is given and everyone partakes
in the broken
body of some life that has been sacrificed
for our hunger,

it is then time to get a praise break *poppin*
like fish grease.
And we can't tell if it's the
100 degree temperature *outside*

or the fire shut up *in* our bones,

but we proceed to dance
right through the flames,
like hell can't touch us any more
than it already has.

And the choir belts out Boosie,
belts out Frankie Beverly & Maze
(*not* Maze featuring Frankie Beverly*)*,
belts out anything Swisher House,
belts out Tucker,
belts out anything bounce, southern soul, or zydeco

louder than the speakers
in perfect harmony
like it done been rehearsed
a million gatherings before.

The testimony of a sweaty top lip shouts,
"YEAHHH!!!"

and not so far in the distance,
a Bud Light can toasts the air
or a red cup full of dat brown toasts the air,
as hands go up and seem to stay there
and wave from side to side as if to testify
that whoever the DJ is,
they have indeed just played *some*body's song.

And the hands and voices keep raisin',
and the asses keep droppin',
scraping the ground like an old Cutlass with a
trunk full of woofers.

And those who can
count the steps to the left
and slides to the right
and hops to the left
and turns to the right,
and *wobble, baby, wobble*
        but never fall down.

And Today, don't no Body feel no ways tired,
      Lord.
And every *able* Body keeps the (heart)beat
until the last second of the song fades
into the next.

And a backyard full of kin/
folks fellowshipping transforms
into a hole in the wall
of Jericho, and every battle
we were worried about the day before
now comes
a-tumblin'
down.

And some days
this is called a *Get Together*
     is called a *Family (Reunion)*
     is called a *Celebration*
     is called *Victory Is Mine*
     is called *Done Got Over*.

Today,
we celebrate
that we are still alive to.
So we go 'head wit our "bad" Self,
and we shake our thangs like tambourines,
like collection plates
begging to be filled
with *change*;
but we just make sure to have 'em
sittin' in the pews
come Sunday morning.

Go to Church on Sunday |

We would carve our initials into ancient, rickety pews
made of the same wood as cheap caskets.
Not even bolted into the floor, they would seesaw slightly
whenever one of the big-boned *"Sisters"*
sat down on your row.
But on the rare occasion when the big-boned woman
sat in front of us, instead, we would carve.

The chipped latex peeled away
like the skin of forbidden fruit,
revealing thick layers
that *tried* to cover thick layers
that *tried* to cover clues as to who sat on that row
however many years before
each time
the building fund could only cover paint.

We studied the letters
and tried to guess whose name they stood for:
Were they still a member?
Or someone long gone?

And were they the same heathen
who stashed the wad of gum,
now hard as knot stuck to tree,
underneath the seat?

We carved quickly and quietly (yet deeply)
as not to have the big-boned Sister
on the row in front of us
turn around and discover the desecration.

"S.M.S."

There.

Now, even if eventually masked as subtle braille
beneath a fresh coat,
there would be evidence that I was here.
Just as I was told I should be.
Every Sunday.
Sitting right on this pew.
Obedient.
Just in case,
one Sunday, I am *not*,
and
God forgets my name.

Good N' Country |

I'm so country, I don't be surprised at all when all this
drawl slip out from between these good n' greasy lips.

So country, I be takin sips of lukewarm tap water from
mason (Dixon) jars,
filled with so much metal, I can still taste the shackle.

Country enough to be sittin on the hoods of broke down
(American-made) cars,
'cuz the yard full of em,
so they must be good for something.

I'm so country, I call all my cousins *"Cousin"*
even though we was raised more like brothers and sisters.

So country, we make sure to be in the House of the Lord
every Sunday,
even when something is wrong, because *whatever it is,*
Jesus can surely fix it.

And we sing the hymns
exactly the way the elders taught us
(even if the words are wrong),
because a *tedious* journey and a *teacher's* journey
both seem like the same kind of hard.

And we eat the peppermint
or the butterscotch
or the strawberry hard candy
from Mother _____'s or Sister _____'s purse,
and say *yes ma'am* and *thank you, ma'am,*
because sweetness should always be
on a country girl's tongue.

The Whole World in His Hands |

I.

A Man's hands were once covered
in car engine oil and pride—
one hand missing a thumb from a day when work
was as hard as expected.

Expert at fixing broken things
except for a family.
Would often disappear beneath the hood
or the engine of sleek bodies
and slide out on his back,
eyes facing God each time.
Hands covered in stubborn stains
that could only be washed away with industrial-strength
soap and the blood of Jesus.

Losing a part of himself
is sometimes the only way man ever learns
to pray.

II.

Another Man's hands were once covered
in gunpowder, some other thing's blood,
and too many secrets.

Somewhere tucked inside a photo album
or a bible, maybe,
is a folded newspaper clipping of him
triumphantly holding a dead two-headed rattlesnake;
and somewhere just outside the frame,

is a smiling group of neighborhood children.
Would often disappear
into the woods and come back with dinner
or another trophy.

Sometimes a man can be hero
to the ones he protects
and hunter to those he abandons in the wild.

III.

Two men.
Two sets of hands.

Stained.
Severed.
But no less whole(ly).

Within them, a world of sacrifices made for
        and of
their own families.

Stay | *For the Children* |

Many nights around this time/ the lullaby of crickets and cicadas is drowned out by the steam/ of two voices boiling behind walls/ thinner than each other's nerves/ and the wind's patience./ A rumbling crescendo/ violently shaking the tiny wood frame house/ and without warning/ a fist slices through the tension in the air/ breaking all that be dam(ned)/ and the two raging rivers bust/ through the bedroom door/ leaving a good night's rest/ and an entire house/ among many other things/ in ruins.

A startling clap of lightning strikes something (maybe a dresser, a chair, a coffee or end table/ maybe flesh and bone)/ into fractured wood and bleeding glass./ Knocks the power out/ in her eyes/ and tries to split/ the whole house in half.

An anger-drunk tornado regurgitates things/ words/ into the air/ with the force of a breeze/ that somebody done pissed off/ as fists and sharp objects and tongues and bodies fly/ everywhere.

Many nights around this time/ what happens in this house is so loud/ it can't stay/ in this house.

Many nights/ a blind band comprised of nothing but cymbals/ marches well into an hour when the lullaby of crickets and cicadas/ should have blended/ into the harmony of brewed coffee and grits with baby birds/ outside/ humming Grace.

And no one hears the aftermath/
the wounded wreckage/
the screaming shadow
the size of a little girl/ in the corner,
crying
and praying/

for one night of peace
and quiet.

Secret **Recipe** |

*And you betta eat **ALL** of it!*

How you gon put all'at on my plate
and expect me to finish it?
Even give me your scraps too?

Tell me that I will grow big and strong,
be fit for Heaven
if I just take one more bite.

Keep it all tucked in the back of my throat,
stuck between my teeth like old rotting meat,
packed tight inside my jaw like Skoal.
Scold my tongue for probin' around in there
to dig it all out.

Tell me to mind my manners,
to not chew with my mouth wide open
so no one can see
what I am being fed.

To shut my lips so tight
they go numb
andmymouthbecomestoofulltowraparound
myownname.

Celie | *The Blk Madonna* |

I. *Juke Joint*

She called me a *virgin*, and I wanted to call her a *blasphema'*, 'cause I knowed what *virgin* mean. I also knowed what somebody climbin on top o' me to "do his bizness" mean.

The man who me and my sista Nettie called *"Our Father"* showed me first. Then a man who name I ain't e'much know til Shug say it first (so I just call him *"Mista"*). They beat it into my bones wit' they mouths and fists and even they bodies, til I forgot that *I* even had a body.

Believed all this body was good for was "*bizness* and birthin babies." So when she say, *"Why Miss Celie... that mean you's still a virgin,"* I remembered that to be Virgin means to be desired—to be praised and worshipped like idol and not to have yo' body used simply as confessional.

Like it be an ugly secret—
    a *shooo*
        issss
            uglyyy
               secret.

Like maybe it be a place for sinners to cum and spill all they moonshine sins.

II. *Sanctuary*

One day I's feelin down, I's feelin mighty low, when She gave me permission to stop hiding behind a closed mouth and pried open legs. To finally see myself the way I came into this world, without burden or shame. To smile big and wide and free of judgement. And that day I seent *me* in that mirror, I knowed there's a God. I knowed that I ain't have to follow no man alive on Earth to find Heaven.

Got me to thinkin' bout Mary—how her body was only used for "bizness" and birthin' babies too. That ain't nobody ever take the time to peel back the Blk & the ugly to find her wings or find her/ angel enough to ever know Heaven even though Mary's body was also needed for everybody to get to Heaven theyself.

(Funny how others will crucify your body to get to a place they don't even find you worthy of bein'.)

III. *A Field of Purple*

Mary, I think about you all the time. Like Sista, you been on my mind. Like I know what it's like to only be worth your weight in what you can do for Man(kind); and how you ain't ask for none of this—not even Joseph's hand in marriage. How even though your name be used by some to lift the heavy of heavenly petitions, or praised only for what you have pushed out (and not pushed back), you still be seen as confessional—as a place for sinners to come and cover you in all of their guilt and sin, but never erasing the holy of you.

And why Mary... that mean you's still a virgin.

Shut That Front Door |

Every woman in my family and in my neighborhood
warned us—

"You bet not let all them flies and mosquitoes in!"

because in, they will come
hovering like Big Brother,
beggin ass buzzards just watchin and waitin
to catch you slippin.

The women with fly-swatters and rolled up newspapers
say them flies be the ones—
inconsiderate and just plain ole disrespectful.
Will circle round yo' face in some kind of suicidal dare.
Will land feet first on a fresh plate
of your favorite meal, with slobbery mouth,
Birdman hand-rubbing over your entree,
knowing damn well they just had dog shit for an appetizer
and ain't even bother to wash they hands
     or wipe they feet
before waltzin' up in yo house to see what all they can get
     dirty.

The women with sometimes nothing
but their bare hands and a good aim
say them mosquitoes be the worst,
because they do not want what is on your plate
but crave what requires the breaking of skin.
Will feast on you without your permission.
Will come with insatiable siphoning mouth

to try and suck
        the life
           right
              out
                  of you.

The women in my family and in my neighborhood
who always got a plate for *just about* everybody
always told me, in so many ways,
that you can't just leave yo' front door wide open
      or else
the swarm will come,
floating in on a welcome you never intended
that they surely plan on wearing out.
Always ready to eat up everything in your house,
but *never* prepared to end up a guest
on the inside

         of

        your

      p   a   l   m.

The Girl and Her Dragon Slayers |

A priestess once told me
that there were men of my bloodline
willing to slay dragons for me.
This I know to be true,
for I have witnessed them battle demons
in the dark and still get up early
to go to work in it.
I know men who know how to hold their liquor
and their tears,
who probably throw up both
when no one is looking.
I know men with arms and tongues like swords,
who can turn wooden houses
into both dungeons *and* castles.
I know kings who wear low-faded [graying] crowns
and little to no gold,
who have reptile skin
and soft hearts,
who often breathe fire[s]
and know
how to extinguish them as well.

A *women* |

I watched my Madear take a few cups of cornmeal, a couple of eggs, a half-gallon of milk, and feed her *entire* family. I watched both my grandmothers take the bitterness of divorce and turn it into some of the *sweetest* homemade cakes you've ever tasted. I watched my own mother take an unplanned teenage pregnancy and years of ridicule and turn it into over 30 years of marriage (and counting), a career in education, and an award-winning poet for a daughter.

I am from a long line of women who know how to take life's most bitter ingredients and turn them into something worth licking your plate for—women whose palms are laced with wrinkles and stardust, who weave miracles from misfortune. You can call them *women*, call them *mothers*, call them *alchemists*, even call them *magicians*. But whatever you call them, just be sure to call them *Ma'am* or *Mrs.*, because they are the type of women who demand respect—no hands on hip or roll of neck to keep you in check; for they are the type of women whose eyes say everything their mouths never need to.

The women in my family inhale life's pollution and exhale gospel. They are walking talking hymnals, perfect verses of chestnut skin and big bones set over organs and strong heartbeats. All testimony and healing. All holy and *how I got over*. The women in my family be bridges over troubled waters—beautiful examples of how to take life's storms and turn them into baptisms.

And some days, I do not feel worthy of this kind of salvation; for I know that I have been saved many times by their blood, sweat, and tears. I often question if I am doing such a legacy any justice. Oh what a cross to bear! Because this world will try to make you forget the strength in your own spine—that it is in your DNA to bend but *never* break. Even after you give and give and give and... never take much for yourself.

For all the times when we are seen as saviors instead of angels, we learn to take the scars on our shoulders and carve out our own wings, which is to say: we don't need the world to tell us we fly (although it would be a nice gesture, well-deserved recognition). Thankfully, our Mamas and MaDears taught us how to be our own tambourines—how to *shake, shake, shake* the devil off our backs and Holy Ghost dance all over his neck. Their Ancestors taught them that.

These are the things that could not be swallowed by the Atlantic Ocean, and for this we say *Hallelujah*. For those who came before us, we say *Thank you, God*. For I am from a long line of women who know how to turn classrooms and kitchens into pulpits—the type of women who have taught me that when your life becomes a sermon that no one else wants to hear, sometimes, you gotta be your own *Amen*.

Grandma's Hands |
After Bill Withers, For Lelia Mae |

Mother. Matriarch. Maker of bomb biscuits and cakes.
A lil bit of butter and a whole lotta Love
being her most important ingredients.
But never was it a secret,
because we all knew what Grandma put in the food
even if we ain't know the *exact* recipe.
Could already taste it long before our mouths
ever knew full.
Always left her house with hearts and bellies to match.

She would always say, *"Now, Grandma ain't got much,"*
not realizing that what she had to give was more
than our stomachs or our hands could ever hold.
Held a special place in her heart
for each and every one of us.
So I'd like to believe that each time she stumbled
over our names:
*"Uh... Shalonda, Sha'Condria, Tawania, Tannell...
You know who I'm talkin to!"*
that was only because she had all of us on her mind.
Her mouth wrapped like a hug around each of our names
in all of her prayers.

Placed an open bible in each room of her house
to show that she served more than just warm meals
and sweet words
(sharp ones if you caused any confusion).
Because as for my Grandma and her house,
the Lord always had a seat at the head of the table.
And for as long as I could remember, she and the rest of
the Disciples would gather around on Thanksgiving Eve—
one stirring the pies, one cleaning the greens,

one peeling potatoes, one shelling the peas,
all of them swapping smiles and *"Ooh Chiles!"*
and the kind of deep-bellied laughter
that only Grandmamas and Mamas and Aunties know
how to reach deep down
and give birth to.
And every year, this became tradition;
became engraved in all our minds and tongues like
scripture.

And faithfully, we recite it like:
For in my Grandmother's house,
there are many memories.
If it were not so, I wouldn't have told you...
about all the random mornings when she would call and
invite us all over,
because she had the sudden urge to make
biscuits from scratch,
scrambled eggs, and pan sausage.
(And of course it wouldn't be right
without the Steen's cane syrup!)
Pineapple upside down, jelly, tea, and pound cakes.
Wrist work to whip the rough side of the batter
into a smooth and creamy calm.
My Grandma had blessed palms
that for decades nursed her family
and a city full of folks back to health
(and Rapides General ain't never had another angel
like her walking its wings since).

Never been afraid to fly.
Would hop on a boat or a plane
or gas up that blue Buick Skylark
(and eventually, that tan Chevrolet Impala)
and hit I-49 North headed for Shreveport

faster than you can spell N-a-t-c-h-i-t-o-c-h-e-s.
Wingspan wide like the doors
of Second Evergreen Baptist Church
or that little brown house on Baldwin Avenue.

Nurse. Usher. Sunday School teacher. Believer.
Bearer of the best popcorn balls.
Sweet Honeybee gathering with the other Queens
on the porch
or at the church
or piling together in somebody's car.
Thick as hives, dripping trails of thick laughter
down roads and highways, spreading Love like pollen.
Her bed/spread, a field of flowers
whenever any/all of us came buzzing around.

Oh, give thanks for the California King mattress
and our Hannah, Louisiana *Queen Majesty*,
master of making us wonder
how one woman could be so many things.
Mother of
Ronnie, Cynthia, Elaine, Steven, Janice, Michael, Jeffrey,
and too many to name.
Came and carried us all here safely in her arms
before returning to the ones
that brought her to us.

My Grandma's hands
clapped in church on Sunday morning.
My Grandma's hands would help heal the sick so well.
My Grandma's hands used to issue words of comfort.
She'd say, *"Things may not be the same.*
But put your faith in Jesus name.
I promise you'll see me again."
My Grandma's hands.

Highest Praise |

My name (with the same number of letters as *Hallelujah*)
is   *Sha'Condria,*

    which sounds a lot like *mitochondria*
    which sounds a lot like *powerhouse of the cell*
    which sounds a lot like *gets shit done*
    which sounds a lot like *creating*
    out of something so small, it can feel like nothing

    which sounds a lot like *mustard seed*
    which sounds a lot like *faith*
    which sounds a lot like *what I believe in*
    is big enough
    which sounds a lot like *even me*

    which sounds a lot like *Love*

    which sounds a lot like
    my name before I came here
    this time
    which sounds a lot like *Before the Before*
    which sounds a lot like
    In the beginning...

        which sounds a lot like a *Word*
        which sounds a lot like a *Breath*

        which sounds a lot like *the Highest Praise.*

To All the Little Black Girls With Big Names |

Whenever someone asks me the meaning of my name, I usually never have an answer. I remember looking for it once in a computer at a shopping mall kiosk, where meanings of names are saved then engraved into keepsakes, thinking all the while that the chances of finding mine would be like the odds of winning the sweepstakes—slim to none. Got tired of people mispronouncing it so I shortened it to "Con," but they *still* got it wrong. Kept confusing me with the lady who once sang that song—*teeelll me sumthin good!* And tell them something I feel I should, so I correct them.

My name is pronounced *sha-**con**-dri-a*. No silent letters. No accents. Preferably pronounced with the drawl of a good ol' Louisiana accent (it just sounds so much sweeter that way). I remember there once was a day when I wished that mother would've stuck to something simple and pret-ty and majestic, like *Tiffany* or maybe even *Alexis*. But my fate was sealed by signatures on my birth certificate, granting me the right to forever bear the shame of having been given a ghetto ass name.

So this here poem is for all the little Blk girls with <u>BIG</u> names.

For the "*-sha*'s" and "*-isha*'s", the "*-ana*'s" and the "*-iqua*'s," who were told to never write their full names on applications, because we live in a nation where your name can tell someone your race or social status. Some think only "dumb ghetto folk" overuse the alphabet. They chalk it up to illiteracy. Never creativity. Or maybe even history.

And I wonder—if those who assume would ever stop to think that maybe... trans-Atlantic submerged native tongues have re-emerged in the form of "ghetto" monikers. Like my little cousin whose name is Tynishia—sounds a lot like *Tinashé*, a name from the Shona tribe meaning *"God is with us."* Or maybe like my friend LaKisha whose name sounds a lot like *Wekesa*, a Bantu name meaning *"born during the harvest."* Or maybe like me. My mother knew that this little girl would be a fighter so she named me Sha'Condria, which sounds a lot like *Shaka*, the great Zulu warrior.

This here poem is for every Daughter

who ever became a professional only to shorten her name to a letter and a period just so phone calls would be returned or higher pay earned, 'cause we all know... don't nobody want an "*-isha*" or an "*-iqua*" to operate on them. But a book can't be judged by its cover nor its title, and the story behind your name can't be contained beneath the tides, so let it rise and take its rightful place on your applications and business cards, desk placards and uniforms until one day "ghetto ass names" become the norm.

But for right now, we're special you see. And there ain't another girl in the world with a name like you or me. So go forth and rep proudly for all the "ghetto-named" girls. And if someone happens to mispronounce your name, make sure to give your neck a swirl, look them right in the eye, and correct them.

My name is pronounced *sha-**con**-dri-a*. Say it right or don't say it at all.

The Filter Says to the Garden |

Scrub off any evidence that you have *actually* lived
    Today.
Don't nobody wanna taste
    the grimy
    the grit
    the journey
on you,

Or smell the musk
or the funk
of everything you've struggled with Today,

Or force their eyes to behold you spotted
    or scarred
    or pitted
    or bruised
    or broken
    or busted
or in any form other than

    flawless.

Don't you know that the only beautiful flowers
are those that smell
of the sweetest ease
    and *look*
like they ain't never *ever* been touched
      by the dirt?

For Lil Kim,
When Being A Regular Blk Girl
Was Not Enuf |

"Being a regular Blk girl wasn't good enough."
—Lil Kim

When I nailed your picture to my Facebook wall
and questioned a Blk woman's attempt to rise
from all of the dead things inside of her,
Kimberly Denise Jones, please forgive me.

For being a part of the social media lynch mob that came
for your neck and your face
when we felt we could no longer recognize you—
unable to see past your pain
like Queen Bees don't know sting.
Like I forgot what it feels like
to not have faith in my own beauty.
Like it is some phantom god. To question its existence.
Believing it to be no "Biggie," knowing damn well
that *he* was part of the problem.

Left you feeling black & ugly as ever, praying
that God would wash your s(k)in away.
Left you wanting to be born *again*.
Left you wanting to *look* like a new creature.

Because *beautiful* can sometimes sound
a lot like speaking in tongues,
especially in a broken language
that tries to leave you the same way.
Plagues you with insecurity
until your natural features begin to feel like leprosy.

Beneath the scars is still a girl with Big Apple lips.
Hair Brooklyn-accent thick.
A nose made perfectly wide enough
to sniff through bullshit.
And Blk/ Go(o)d skin.

And we are re-minded (to give thanks),
even when everything about us feels heavy
and not Light enough. Especially this skin.
Even when we feel like *too much* and *not enough*
at the *same* damn time.

Strong has become so much a part of our names,
how easy we forget
that we are malleable, molded of flesh and blood,
and not of stone.
That we are made in the image of monuments that have
already been nipped and tucked by colonizing hands.
That even if we too chisel away at the ones
in which we live, we must consider
that the dust will *always* return
in the faces of our Daughters.

And we cannot teach them to recite/sing along
with false doctrine
blasted over the airwaves about how Becky
With the Good Hair is blessing/sacrament.
Cannot make habit our addiction
to overdosing on her communion.
Will not survive if we *drown*
our Daughters in images that look nothing like them
and call it *baptism*.

Cannot pass on the partaking of our own broken bodies
and call it *being made whole again*.

Or be the Ones *doing* the breaking.

Or shed our own blood and call it *work/werk*.

Or show Daughter, by example, to crucify Herself
daily in bathroom mirrors, and still rise
with every Sun/day
mo[u]rning,
having saved everyone
but Herself.

God Bless The Child |
An assignment from Mama Fiyah

Dearest Sha'Condria,

You deserve to not care so much about what your school pictures look like. Instead, let your lips become open shutter—within them, an unapologetically snagga-toothed smile. Do *not* hide. Do *not* be ashamed of anything you have ever lost, because that same smile is proof that everything you need *always* comes back.

You deserve to fly. To *be* fly. To rock too-many-plastic-Goody-barrettes-to-count in your hair. You deserve to do the most, to "get carried away." To run freely outside and have them be the only thing to ever smack you across your face. You deserve to only know sweet penny candy, sticky frozen cup type Love—the kind that stay in yo teeth and on your fingers 'til you choose to wash it away.

Today is the day you release yourself to stretch & breathe & *not* walk a tightrope of pins and needles in this soft body. Do not be afraid/ashamed of the girl in you. Or the *tomboy* in you. Love it *all* as whole and as living as Earth; for it knows how to take care of *itself.* How the body sends scars as a reminder of how beautiful healing can be (depending on how you look at it). Bask in your own wonder. Feel buoyancy in this body, and never know it as anchor. Breathe in this body and feel no shame about what it was created to *Be*, nor about whatever it will never become.

The world is not your fault. Even though yo mama had you young, you ain't never been a mistake. But you be the right answer to *everything*. You are your *own* prayer, whispered from the bottom of yo mama's fifteen-year old belly and bellowed into existence long before *you* ever had a tongue. Long before anyone ever taught you to pronounce your name *Burden*. So shake that load off girl, and give thanks for the day yo mama and daddy slipped up and you slipped out—you, Legacy that others tried to name *Embarrassment*.

You, little girl with the *big* name, seesaw smile, face full of your daddy's sisters, and faith the size of a family tree. You deserve to believe in the scripture inscribed into your skin, and to give thanks for remembering to hold yourself tighter than anything else in *this* world.

Love, *You*.

The Gospel of Girls Who 'Do' Hair |
an Edge/People-Snatching Word

Ain't they somethin, these hands?
These magical Blk girl hands—how they can weave
protective prayers into weary scalps...
literally?
Abra-ca-dab a lil Blue Magic into our palms,
          and *poof!*
all of your day's worries *and* nappy edges are gone.

This kind of honor is our birthright, passed down
from our grandmamas.
Us sittin on kitchen floor or in kitchen chair,
watchin MawMaw stand over gas stove
and wave hot pressing comb like wand—
all of that smoke and fire!

This kind of tradition is our apprenticeship
that crossed over on ships—
how within chained-together palms,
we still managed
to carry the muscle memory of gripping edges
and trying our damnedest not to go over them
(not unless that was the only way back Home).

Some say
that hair-braiders in many ancient cultures
were considered healers—
those with access to the head, to the crown chakra.
I guess that's why my grandmama always say,
"Be careful who you let get in your head.
Tell 'em don't throw that shed hair away,
for fear a bird will make nest of it

and drive you crazy someday."
Instead remember
the smoke and fire in yo' grandmama's hand,
make ash of the hair, and return it
to the dust from which it came, like *poof...*

Watch a magic Blk girl sittin' on the front porch
       or in the front room
       or in the kitchen
       or in the beauty shop
teach a whole ass history lesson
about how this entire country was built,
using nothing but her hands.

Braiding patterns into hair so we do not forget
the way to Freedom.
Tired aching feet from standing all day.
Arthritic hands balled up into a fist
like *kitchens,*
                resisting.

Greasy finger griot who do business by word
of mouth, the same way our people share
all things we consider sacred.

She who has mastered the art
of catching and gripping
that which other folk let slip
right through their fingers.
Hair savior, walking on waves across continents
of coils to create culture out of cuckabugs.
Expert in *Economics 101—*
that is, how to take nothing
(i.e. *your edges*)
and turn them into something,

And ain't they somethin?

These old testament hands—how they make
Red Sea of parts?
These ancient Kemetic hands—how they make
perfect geometry of box braids?
DNA kinky-twisting good hair into our genetics
since Genesis; and the Good Word
on the street be that each time a Blk woman slays
your edges, an angel gets its baby hair.

Giver of a new do and a new life.
Folk be born again
when they leave our chairs
or from in between our knees—
they both be a heaven
this world don't even deserve.
For heavy is the head that wears a tangled crown,
but anointed are the hands that tend
the tender and itchy scalps and know
how to build an entire kingdom
from scratch.

*Her*ricane |

I have survived many
      a season
where I was a perfect mix
of sweltering passion
      and cold shoulder,
attracting lovers who
         like me
     were the same kind
     of storm—

         the kind that ain't never laid eyes
         on a beautiful,
               calm sky
         it did not wish
to crack   wide   open.

When Being Interviewed
on the Red Carpet on Judgment Day
and Asked What I Am Wearing |

I stand before myself
every day,
take up the gavel,
and use it to beat myself into
worthy/presentable.

Pummel myself beyond recognition
until I look in the mirror
and can no longer see me.
Til I am covered in Blood.
Til I begin to believe that Punishment
looks much better on me than Truth.

Punishment is my Sunday's best,
and why this old thing, Truth
is just some expensive tailored suit that I wear
underneath a cheap costume
      to the club
      to the bar
      to the heaux/crack/trap house
      to bed
      to any other place
they told me
God wouldn't dare
step foot in.

Until the Sun Shows Up
to Crash the Party |

Our bodies   still thirsty
swamp together beneath a dark
liquor sky poured over distant stars and Cajun moon.
It is obvious we both have a drinking problem—
the way we crash into each other like broken
        glass and call it a *toast*.

Cheers to you always showing up to my pity
parties   uninvited   right after you leave
the club, wearing your own familiar sweat
and bringing with you as a plus-one
        the salt of other oceans.

Still,
        I always make room.

Empty my insecurities down my own throat
til I become a hollowed
shot glass that not even your entire body
could fill. Your drunken breath,
a hot and sweaty slow grind,   making
the inside of my ears *and* my thighs, a sloppy pour.
I make VIP section of my sofa, my bed,
bottle service of my own body,
and you drink until you are no longer able
        to drive yourself home.

So often we make dancefloor of my apartment
        until I start to believe
that you have mistaken it for *home*,
or at least a place where you can play

all of your favorite songs. We spin
like heads—each other's skin turntables
beneath our tongues, both of us lost
                in the grooves.

The mixtape you scratch into my head
            got me
movin' my hips like ain't nobody watchin.
Got me liftin my hands
            and my feet
                    and my ass
high in the air
toward a roof
        that we both came to set on fire.

And over all this crackling blaze,
        I swear I hear you say
that you want to give your daughter   my smile.

But we are both faded, along with the music.

The room, now rotating non-stop
                    on a wobbly axis
                    in the darkness
and all we can see are the stars,
            hungover;

I am no longer beaming.

Can feel the strings once holding me up
wearing off, along with all the drinks we had
on the house.
Both of us now wrapped in a heavy blanket
        of regret, swimming in
humidity thick as a Fat Tuesday crowd
        sticky as a Bourbon Street bar top

sweaty as palms glued to a daiquiri cup
    melting
        pouring
           spilling into the mouth
             of the next
             morning,
and the light crawls in
        and hurts

                our eyes.

Know/Do Betta |

And all this time
I thought it was *them* that I didn't trust.

Let them tell me that feeling I had deep down in my gut
was just the bruises left from the kind, "loving"
fists that came before them.
Even convinced myself the same.
Even when I saw their once-open hand go full clinch.
Turned my cheek,
but the sucker punch landed anyway
right square in my intuition.

Screamed as they walked away
leaving me to nurse my own broken ribs,
always saying to myself:
I already saw it coming.
Painted the first red flag my favorite color green.
Painted every one after that yellow instead
of uprooting them altogether.

But no one wants to hear the wincing or the whining
of a girl covered in bandaids.
They will just call her *clumsy*.
Say something must be wrong with *her*
for bleeding *so* much.
We, humans, do not like to look down
at our own bruised knuckles.
Never like to take accountability
for the bloody work of our own hands.

Too many times, I (and all who are enviously watching)
have been distracted from the slaughter

by magic trick
        by rabbit out of the hat
        by expensive costume
        by gifts and good deeds.
Too many times, they have replaced the person
they intro-/se- duced me to
with a ghost
then told me that I was seeing things.

Called my *Common Sense* out of its name.
Called it *Jealous* and *Insecure* like they ain't change
their own name from *Liar*
to *Too Good to Be True*.

And all this time
I thought it was *them* that I didn't trust.

Like my body ain't been with me all these lifetimes,
protecting/warning me of impending danger.
Like my fight or flight ain't tell me to jet
the fuck up outta there the first time.
Like I ain't hear my racing heart telling me
to run.
Like my belly ain't *been* bloated
with bullshit.
Like *this* shoulda been the time that I bit the hand
that caressed me at night.
Like that fluttering feeling in my stomach wasn't
butterflies, but instead,
was the muscles bracing themselves for a blow
that I know
I felt coming
ever since
Hello.

Hoarder |

Expired feelings./ A giant pile of origami./ Faded receipts for things/ that (you) will never return./ Never been too good at letting go of things./ Remember the 1st grade game of tug-of-war during P.E./ Burned so much/ everyone else released their grip/ on the rope/ but you held on./ The inside of your palms, red and raw/ like holding a bleeding heart./ You learned Love that day./ Memories stored in a box of moldy outdated newspapers/ or a tangled mountain of Christmas lights./ An obstacle course of coded language./ House so full of ghosts/ no one can enter/ and you refuse to leave./ One heartbreak shy of being buried alive./ Television cameras and film crew show up as an intervention./ The mess captured on film and aired across world./ Others with their own clutter twist their guilty faces/ disgusted/ asking (like they don't know) how / it ever got this bad./ You look around and remember/ the rope burns and calluses inside your hands/ that have been there since 1st grade/ and you finally let go/ the habit of holding on to useless things/ even if it hurts more than the fear/ of losing everything/ you thought you needed.

(Miss) America |

Prized possession and pedestal-ready
    at Birth.

The fathers who founded you
molded you
  in their phallacies.
Already gathering ammunition and rope
the moment the ultrasound showed you
  suspended from umbilical cord,
a rotten apple swinging
      not at all far from the tree.

You were *still*   born,
  covered in deadly sins.

It's a...
sacrifice made of someone *else's* child!
And so goes the belief that someone *else's* blood
is enough to change your name
    to Redeemed.

Tongue hell enough to burn Rosewoods
(in)to the ground,
  crying wolf enough to fill countless graves
    with your tears.

Your reflection, a lie painted
  as beauty standard.
Your name, a *Dream*
  that stays trending,
sold at a price that no one

other than thieves can afford,
  makes economy out of culture
        and genocide.

An entire world eating/starving
  from the palm of your hands, not realizing
        how dirty your hands truly are.

Blk Friday Preyer |

Today, the cash registers chime
like church bells to commemorate
the People as they celebrate

and give thanks for the boats and the blankets
and the bullets and the bricks and the bars.
Say grace over the extermination and offer
up praise that the growling
only exists *outside* the stomach,

today.

Because some folks ain't got nothin
but a mouth full of prayer and spit
to swallow
and nowhere warm or safe
to lay their heads.

At least you now have so many
boxes to unwrap
to keep you
on your knees for lifetimes to come.

A Seat at the Table |

Nah.
To hell with that.
I heard they don't even wash they hands
(unless it is of the blood).
They got a kitchen, filthy
and full of secrets;

and

the food ain't really *that* good
or good *for* you
no way.

Besides,

      my Mama already anointed my head
       with grease.
      My cup runneth over
       with my Grandmama's homemade eggnog.
      And *Goodness* and *Mercy* be following me
      like they my closest homies,
      around every hood
      (that now all feel like heaven),
           all the days of my life.

      And I will dwell
      in the House of my Daddy
      and sit at the table
      my Ancestors already *(pre)*paid
      for me
      in the presence of my enemies.
         Forever.

Blk Crack |

I'm not sure who first said that it don't,

     but Blk *do* crack.

In fact,

Blk crack so much
     til it's often etched in smoke stains
     all over Blk lips.

Blk got smile lines hollowed out by pain—
     a void filled with laughter, filled with punchlines
     from the best ribbing sessions
     and *"Yo mama"* jokes.

Blk crack so much til it ain't to be tried,
     ain't to be played with.

Blk crack til its heels become hardened
     from marching and making
     our dance look more like entertainment
     than ritual, than prayer.

Blk got wrinkles and dimples and stretch marks
     and dark marks and scars
     and gashes and lashes
     and keloids,

     got gangrene
     and rope burns
     and spines sprouting
     chokecherry trees,

got gaping holes   the size of everything

     the devil stole.

Blk *do* crack.
Dries up like raisin
     but ain't never been afraid of the Sun.

Blk *do* crack.
     Sometimes, busts wide open;
     but never does it break.

Even when the sky or this world does,
Blk gon *still* be here
 still smiling
 still laughing
 still dancing
     still living
 still looking

nothing
like what it done

     been through.

[1]N----- |

You *too* **Blk**.

Like
ain't came over here with a passport *or* a visa **Blk**.
Like *too* bottom of the cargo ship **Blk**.
Too bottom of the Atlantic **Blk**.
Too bottom of the melting pot **Blk**.

You the kinda **Blk** ain't never *really* been
nowhere—

one foot stuck in a plot of land
that carries your blood
        but someone else's name,
the other foot anchored in your *own* forgetful
mouth.

You *too* loud **Blk**—

a **Blk** that everything that wishes to be **Blk**
tries to swallow.
Everybody else wanna tell *your* story **Blk**.
Wanna sing *your* song
and not call it karaoke **Blk**.
Mimic your cool and disregard
        all the scorching, red summers
                that made you *this* **Blk**.

You *too* bottom of the space|ship **Blk**—
a **Blk** this world can't even be|hold;

a **Blk** *so* Infinite,
when you are told to go *back*
where you came from,
you know that means

    EVER/yw/HERE.

---

[1]**nebula** neb·u·la /ˈnebyələ/ (noun): mist; fog; a giant cloud
of dust and gas in space that can come from the gas and
dust thrown out by the explosion of a dying star; nursery
for new stars; they play a crucial role in the chemical
evolution of the galaxy.

All Our Medicine |

"We have all our medicine right here, right here."
—*All Our Medicine*,
a song passed through oral/aural tradition
from Deirdre Smith to Randolph Carr to Kei Slaughter

The day I heal, they will not be here.
Not the wielder of every weapon formed
against me,
of every dis-ease,
of every greedy imagination.
Not even those with ropes and
bullets and fire stashed
away in the dark corners of their colorblind
eyes and token-pickin' teeth.

Never will their leeching mouths know the sweet
sav(i)or of my scars.
Not the covetous vultures who beg
to taste/ to devour my whole
beauty again
and again and again and...
until my bones are nothing
more than crumbs scattered beneath their table.
I will no longer offer up
my body as a living sacrifice for bellies
already swollen full.

I will hold my *own* blood
and my *own* Truth
on my *own* tongue—
a canon of Testaments/testimonies,

telling how I already mastered
walking on oceans of unspeakable memories
without having to fear *their* god.

Because neither fear *nor* their god ain't
never been here.
Ain't never stepped foot on this
boundless body of holy land, spun from something
much holier out in the ether.
Ain't never basked in a glow
wide as all of Existence.
Begat from an inconceivable darkness.
Begat from a muzzled mouth that
still musters up the might to speak:

So... *let there be*

this great *big* Light of mine.
I'm gonna let it shine like spit
mixed with mud to make a blind man see,
like salve glistening in my Grandmama's tallow jar,
like balm to make whole
a wound deep enough to carry the suffering
of *too* many Gileads.

    The/To- day that I am *already* healed,
    their god will be nowhere to be found.

    Only *my* God will be
    Everywhere,
    receiving *all* the Glory.

I

My scars do not tell
my *whole* story.

You cannot look at them
only
and assume you know
my name.

Recessional|

As my grandmother **Frankie Mae** says at every Sunday service, *"First giving honor to God, to whom all honor is due..."* Thank you to that same grandmother who has braved every storm beautifully, unbending in her belief in that which lies *"somewhere over the rainbow."* Mama, *"I will always Love you."*

To the two teenagers who had to learn early (through trial and error) how to be parents, my Mama and Daddy, **Tawania** and **Steven**, who may not have always understood or known exactly what I was doing/becoming, but who have always given me room to find out. Although the road has been very rocky at times, we have still found a way to build a church upon it. Your Love is one of my greatest testimonies.

To *all* of my family on both sides—the **Sices, Brown**, **Walker**, **Payton**, **Bowman**, **Thomas**, and **Sibley** families (and all my other *Blk* ancestral lines)—my Loving grandfathers, grandmothers, uncles, aunts, greats, cousins... I couldn't have picked better tribes. May our roots be repaired, and our branches continue to grow, unbound.

To **Mya**, who I Love like a daughter until I someday have my own. May you be an answered prayer for the world, and may you grow to be your own most resounding *Amen*.

To the place of my birth, **Pineville**, my hometown of **Alexandria** and my beloved home-hood, the **Sonia Quarters**, thank you for being hard but good ground.

To all my friends (you know who you are). To anyone I have ever Loved, even those who may not have always Loved me back. To every teacher who shared knowledge and wisdom beyond a curriculum. To everyone who has ever supported my words and my work. To anyone who has ever offered me a stage or a platform. To my **Alexandria Museum of Art Rhythm & Rhymes** and **Southern Fried** families. To my **New Orleans** community and arts family, especially **Team SNO** (*especially* the original squad—**Tank, Keem, Kat,** and **Quess?**), **Pass It On, Pozazz,** and **Ashe Cultural Arts Center**, thank you for being a home, for allowing me space in your city, in your hearts, and for giving me a [new] name.

To my sister, my bestie, my editor, my publisher, my advisor, my ear most times when nobody else but God will listen, **Asia Rainey-Ani** (Iya Ifatola Oyagbemi). We ain't the kind to brunch and go get our nails did, but we are the kind who always build and manifest bold dreams together. Thank you for helping me to *"shut up and fly."*

To **All the Little Blk Girls With Big Names,** no matter what the world tries to call you (or tries to convince you to call yourself), always, *always* remember that your name is indeed *Holy*. Answer to nothing less.

I Love you *All*, and there is absolutely nothing you can do about it.